Overcoming Persecution

by
Annette Capps

13th Printing 2018
Over 110,000 in print

Overcoming Persecution
ISBN 978-1-937578-32-9
Formerly titled: Understanding Persecution
ISBN 13: 978-0-9747513-3-7
Formerly ISBN 13: 978-0-89274-214-1
Copyright © 1982 by Annette Capps
P.O. Box 10, Broken Arrow, Oklahoma 74013

Overcoming Persecution

Among the spiritual principles in the Bible, there are many statements made about the laws of sowing and reaping, the results or end punishment of wicked living, and the results or rewards of righteous living. The Word of God speaks truth to our hearts about every avenue of living so that we will not be shocked or surprised by anything that confronts us.

We know that we are more than conquerors through Christ Jesus; but occasionally we fail to realize that in order to be a conqueror, there must be something or someone to conquer and overcome.

One of the areas in life that we must learn to overcome is persecution. Of course, I recognize that there are different degrees of persecution. Here in the United States, for instance, we have not experienced the kind of persecution experienced by Christians in other countries. But the

Word of God does not give us different principles for overcoming these varying degrees of suffering by persecution.

Jesus suffered much persecution in His ministry, even to the point of being executed by His enemies. But was He overcome by it? No! He arose victorious over death, hell, and the grave. Neither did He let it affect His life and attitudes. Even at the cross, He cried out for forgiveness for His enemies.

How did He do it? Let's look at some statements Jesus made early in His ministry.

Blessed are they which are persecuted for righteousness' sake.

Matthew 5:10

Jesus always said what He meant and meant what He said. After all, He spoke only the words He heard His Father speak. He said, *Blessed* are they which *are* persecuted. Blessed. How could He say that? How could a person be blessed by being persecuted? Certainly the person who is persecuting another is not pronouncing blessings on him! The word *blessing* means favor, benefit, and fortunate.

If you are being persecuted, you must be in favor with God because of righteousness. Those who persecute are not in favor with God because of their unrighteousness.

Jesus continues:

Blessed are ye, when men shall revile you, and persecute you, and shall say all manner of evil against you falsely, for my sake.

Matthew 5:11

Before we continue, we need to take note of this verse. You are blessed when people speak evil against you falsely. Jesus did not say you are blessed when they speak the truth about you. Only a person who is living righteously can truly be persecuted in the manner Jesus taught, i.e., for righteousness' sake. If you are living unrighteously and are guilty of the accusations, then you are simply reaping what you have sown. So living righteously will bring persecution.

The Nature of Persecution

Most people approach the subject of persecution from a very negative standpoint. They say, "I'm just suffering for Jesus."

But persecution is not a negative subject. The Word of God tells us that godly living will cause us to suffer persecution (2 Timothy 3:12). To make such a statement is not anti-faith; it's just a fact. (Some Christians have been persecuted without even knowing it.) However, the Word of God also says that faith overcomes persecution.

To be persecuted for righteousness' sake means for being righteous and for walking uprightly in the uncompromising Word of God.

Jesus did not say, "Blessed are they which are persecuted for unrighteousness' sake." You are not blessed for living unrighteously, nor are you blessed when rebuked for sin. You are blessed when men revile you and persecute you and say all manner of evil against you falsely for Jesus' sake.

You can still overcome persecution suffered because you sinned, but the Word of God says that you are blessed when men speak all manner of evil against you falsely.

Why Persecution?

There are several reasons for persecution:

1. Righteousness
2. Pride
3. Jealousy
4. Religious Spirits

1. Righteousness

Jesus said there will be persecution for righteousness' sake. He was not making a "bad confession" or a negative statement; He was simply warning us so that we could count the cost of following Him.

Why would anyone want to persecute a believer who is trying to walk according to the Word of God?

The answer is simple: The light of God that is in a righteous person exposes the darkness in others, and it makes them extremely uncomfortable. The truth is they can't stand it because it reveals the wickedness in them. If you were covered with dirt and grime, you certainly wouldn't want to stand next to someone dressed in clean, white clothing. It's too much of a contrast.

Men love darkness rather than light because their deeds are evil (John 3:19). If sinners keep company with other sinners, they don't look quite so bad!

I have been around some people who did not feel comfortable to be in the same room with me - not because I am superspiritual; but because of the life, the light, and the righteousness of God that is in me. That light exposed their evil deeds (to them) and convicted them of their sin.

If people are uncomfortable around you, it is probably because the Light is shining through you. That Light reveals all their sins. If they are religious, their "dirty clothes" - the filthy rags of their self-righteousness - will be exposed.

Once after having a perfectly good day, I stepped into a fast-food restaurant and ordered a hamburger with mustard (no onions!). The man behind the counter put my sandwich in a sack and said, "That'll be $1.85." When I paid him, he took my change out of the cash register and threw it at me! I had to pick it up off the floor.

I thought, God, *what's* wrong *with* me? I *didn't* do *anything* to him.

God said, "The light in you exposes the darkness in him."

Even in a restaurant, without a word said about God, that Light was shining, revealing and exposing.

The light and life of God shone through evangelist Smith Wigglesworth and exposed the darkness in others, even as he rode passenger trains. God's presence in him caused people to fall on the floor, screaming out, "God save me! I'm a sinner!"

2. Pride

Another cause of persecution is pride.

When the light comes, people realize they are wrong; but because of their pride, they don't want to admit they have been in darkness.

Those who have been blinded by the god of this world (the Devil) are not guilty of spiritual pride because they have not chosen of their own will to remain in darkness. It's just that they have never been enlightened.

In John 9:39-41 Jesus said:

"For judgment I am come into this world, that they which see not might see; and that they which see might be made blind.

And some of the Pharisees which were with him heard these words, and said unto him, Are we blind also?

Jesus said unto them, If ye were blind, ye should have no sin: but now ye say, We see; therefore your sin remaineth. "

These Pharisees did not want to admit that they had been in the dark because it would have been an embarrassment to them. It would have hurt their pride. After all, they *were* the religious leaders of the day! They would rather stay in darkness than come to the light and admit that they had been wrong. They would rather persecute Jesus and kill Him (put out the Light) than change.

Not long ago, I heard an evangelist tell a story about the pastor of a church in which he had preached the Word for a week. Before the evangelist left that church, the pastor said to him, "I recognize that what you have been preaching is the truth; but I'd rather die than admit I've been wrong all these years."

Shortly thereafter, that man fell dead in his pulpit. Why? Because of pride. The light came and the darkness of religious doctrine was exposed, but pride would not let him admit that he had been wrong.

3. Jealousy

Jealousy over Christians' blessings is also a cause of persecution.

When my family was struggling to make a living as farmers in Arkansas - having our crops destroyed by hail, stretching to make ends meet, wondering what we were going to do next - no one persecuted us. They just felt sorry for us. They certainly weren't jealous of what we had!

I remember when my dad would say, "If I planted a cotton seed on top of a fence post and it came up, a weed would grow up beside it and choke it out!"

His confession ruled our finances and ruined them.

When I would say, "Daddy, I want a new coat for school," he would answer, "New coat? We don't even have the money to buy a new toothbrush! We're never going to make it. Everything I touch falls apart. I don't know why. I just can't seem to do anything right. "

(My father, Charles Capps became a successful minister of the Gospel and author of the best-selling book, *The Tongue, A Creative Force.* He learned!)

At that point in our lives, we had no problem with persecution!

In Mark, chapter 10, Peter said to Jesus, *Lo, we have left all, and have followed thee* (v. 28).

Jesus answered him with these words:

"Verily I say unto you, There is no man that hath left house, or brethren, or sisters, or father, or mother, or wife, or children, or lands, for my sake, and the gospel's, But he shall receive an hundredfold now in this time, houses, and brethren, and sisters, and mothers, and children, and lands, with persecutions; and in the world to come eternal life (vv. 29-30)."

Somebody may ask, "Does that hundred fold mean everyone will have a million dollars, expensive cars, and a mansion to live in?"

No the idea is that you will be provided for, you can prosper in this life and not have to scratch the bottom of the bucket at the end of every month!

There is a stipulation, however, for receiving the hundredfold return: You *will receive it* **with persecutions** (v. 30). Without a doubt, persecutions will come.

When my family tapped into the Word of God and began to prosper as Jesus promised, an *hundredfold in* this *lifetime* - houses, land, cotton, soybeans, rice - then many people became jealous. They got mad and persecuted us because we were being blessed.

Some accused us of getting our money by questionable means. They believed if you were truly a Christian, you would be poor or barely getting along. They misquoted the scriptures "Money is the root of all evil." It is the "love of money" that is the root of all evil (1 Timothy 6:10). Some have had the idea that all rich people are wicked, but the Bible doesn't teach that!

Wouldn't it be wonderful if people upon seeing others prospering and being blessed, said, "I'll bet they're Christians!" The Word of God teaches that *the wealth of the sinner is laid up for the just* (Prov. 13:22).

Are **you** just? Are **you** ready to receive?

4. Religious Spirits

Another cause of persecution is religious spirits. When religious spirits are operating, you will see jealousy, pride, and self-righteousness.

This is why Jesus was so persecuted when He was here on earth. The sinners really were not the ones who persecuted Him; they came, were healed, then supported Him. The people who persecuted Jesus were the ones who thought they had the light; but their "enlightenment" was really darkness.

Your relatives and friends might have spoken ugly of you, saying things like: "Speaking in tongues - that's of the Devil! Did you hear about her? She's caught up with that charismatic bunch that believes the Bible is the Word of God. Every time you see her, she's muttering to herself. She even reads the Bible when she's not in church and believes in praying for the sick. How could an intelligent person do that?

Don't feel alone! People said that John the Baptist was demon possessed. They didn't like it because he wouldn't drink anything strong or join in with their New Year's Eve party!

Do you know what they said about Jesus? His relatives said He was *beside himself* (Mark 3:21). Because He went to sinners' houses and ate, the religious people called Him a winebibber and a glutton (Matthew 11:19). They even accused Him of being demon possessed (Luke 11:15).

You can't please everyone. Unless you agree with everyone else's ideas of what is correct, someone will probably say you are beside yourself or not in your right mind. Jesus did what he saw the Father do and it did not agree with the Pharisees theology.

If they said these things about Jesus, why would they say anything different about you? You have the same Light in your spirit.

The Source of Persecution: Satan

Though there are several different causes of persecution, there is only one source: Satan.

In Revelation 12:10, we are told that Satan is the accuser of the brethren. God is not the accuser of the Church or Christians. People who continually accuse Christians are siding with the Devil, even though they often don't know it.

Though Satan is the source of all persecution, he attacks in two ways: through demon spirits or through the people he influences.

Demon Spirits

A good example of satanic persecution through demon spirits is the account of

Paul's thorn in the flesh (2 Corinthians 12:1-9). Paul's thorn in the flesh was a messenger sent from Satan to buffet, or harass, him. Paul said this harassment came because of the abundance of revelations he had received. (v. 7.)

Everywhere Paul went to preach, the Devil stirred up people against him. Satan wanted to stop Paul from sharing and preaching the revelations he had received from the Lord.

In the book of Acts, there is the account of a woman with a spirit of divination who was used of the Devil to hinder Paul's ministry (Acts 16:16-18).

Most of us have probably experienced satanic persecution to one degree or another; but I think ministers probably experience it to a greater degree because, above all things, the Devil does not want the Gospel preached. Therefore, he brings harassments to hinder the effectiveness of a ministry. Let me give you two good examples.

The first occurred to me when there was a strike by air controllers. I was the opening-night speaker for a four-day convention in San Diego. Because of the strike, the airline company could not tell me whether or not my flight would be cancelled, so we decided to fly my plane.

The first problem we encountered was finding maps for the trip. (This was before electronic maps and GPS.) Nearly everyone was out of maps, and it took several hours to locate the ones we needed for the trip.

Then there were several boxes, too large to carry, that had to be shipped. Finally, after searching for an hour to find a store open where we could buy tape to secure the boxes, we packed the car and drove to the airport.

When we arrived, we found that the plane still had not been pulled out of the hangar or filled with fuel. After another delay, we were off the ground and everything seemed fine. However, after an hour or so in the air, I noticed that one of the radios was acting strange. Within a few seconds, all of the radios and most of the electrical equipment quit completely. So we had to return home, flying with an alternator out.

I recognized that this was harassment of the enemy, and I refused to act in frustration. By the time I arrived in San. Diego, however, I had been given several opportunities to rejoice in persecution!

The second example was a situation that happened to my father. During a hot summer while Dad was still farming and ministering part-time, he had four tractors with air- conditioned cabs. Within only a short period of time, all four air conditioners quit working. Then the air conditioner in his truck went out; and at the house, the central air unit had broken. One day when Mother and Dad got into their car, the air conditioner in it wouldn't work!

A few days later they were on the way to a speaking engagement when the plane's air conditioner failed. When they landed, a gentleman picked them up at the airport in a car that had a broken air conditioner.

Dad held a three-day seminar in that city in the heat because the air conditioner in the auditorium had quit working! (I know this sounds ridiculous - it was! But it's true. I was around when part of this happened.)

A week or so later after a rest at home, they left for another meeting. When they checked into the hotel, they had to change rooms three times because the air conditioner didn't work in two of them! To get away from their hot room, they went to a restaurant to eat. While there, all the power in the restaurant went out - lights, air conditioning, everything!

When telling this story, my father said, "And then my lightning-fast mind caught on! We were being harassed by a demonic spirit."

When he and Mother went back to the hotel, they rebuked that spirit by saying, "In the name of Jesus Christ of Nazareth, I command you to get out of here and leave me alone! You'll not touch another air conditioner where I'm going!"

After that declaration the harassment stopped. You see, the Devil is not nearly as powerful as he would have us believe. His purpose is to stop the Gospel from being preached or keep you from hearing it. If he was so powerful, he would have kept my dad from ministering. Because he couldn't do it, he just tried to harass and frustrate him.

You may have encountered harassment when going to a meeting. That's because a messenger of Satan* was sent to hinder you from receiving the Word. The Devil doesn't want you to receive any higher revelations. He doesn't want you to find out how powerful you can be.

People Influenced by Satan

You need to watch out in two different areas:

1. When Satan continually uses one person to harass you.

---

*   For more on this subject read Charles Capps' book *"Triumph Over the Enemy."*

2. When he uses one person to bring strife and contention among Christians.

The Word of God tells us:

For we wrestle not against flesh and blood, but against principalities, against powers, against the rulers of the darkness of this world, against spiritual wickedness in high places.

Ephesians 6:12

When an individual is continually used to harass you, recognize that it is a plan of the enemy to frustrate you and cause you to lose your effectiveness. Just recognizing what is happening will help. Then deal with the matter in the spirit realm - in prayer and intercession.

If one person brings confusion again and again, you must bind the spirit that is influencing him. You can't grab the person by the neck and say, "I bind you in the name of Jesus!" but you can take authority over the evil spirit that is using him and command it to leave.

Christians have been wrestling against

each other, instead of against the powers of darkness. That allows strife to enter in, causing confusion, contention, and every evil work. Through strife, Satan has tried to get the members of the Church to persecute each other.

Victory Over Persecution

If anybody knows how to overcome persecution, Jesus does! He was persecuted more than anybody else, but He overcame it.

Know You Are Blessed

Blessed are they which are persecuted for righteousness' sake: for theirs is the kingdom of heaven.

Matthew 5:10

How can you be blessed when you are being **persecuted?** Doesn't that sound strange?

In Luke 6:22 Jesus said:

Blessed are ye, when men shall hate

you, and when they shall separate you from their company, and shall reproach you, and cast out your name as evil, for the Son of man's sake.

Blessed are you when people are spreading rumors about you. Blessed are you when people are lying about you.

You will get extra special rewards if you are persecuted. In Matthew 5:12 Jesus said, ... *for great is your reward in heaven: for so persecuted they the prophets which were before you.*

Rejoice!

The key to overcoming persecution is to rejoice. In the first part of Matthew 5:12, Jesus said, *Rejoice,* and be *exceeding glad.* He begins Luke 6:23 with these words:

Rejoice ye in that day.

"Hallelujah! Thank You, Jesus! Glory to God! That's what You told us to do, Jesus! We are to rejoice and be glad!"

Why would you be glad when people are stirring up all manner of evil against you? Because you know you are doing the right thing. If you weren't, people would probably leave you alone.

Why did they persecute the prophets? Because the prophets spoke the truth of God's Word. Their righteousness exposed the unrighteousness of the people. You are doing the right thing too when you are obedient to God Who sees your right living.

Beware! Devilish Enlightenment!

You are to rejoice when you are being persecuted for righteousness' sake, but make sure the persecution is really happening.

Jesus said to take heed lest the light (or enlightenment) in you be darkness. (Luke 11:35.)

James talks about a superficial wisdom (or enlightenment) that is earthly and unspiritual, even devilish. James 3:14 in The *Amplified Bible* says it produces envy, strife, jealousy, and contention.

This devilish enlightenment causes a false sense of persecution: a persecution complex.

I am sure you have experienced feeling as though someone were talking about you. Someone *looks* your way and *whispers. Suddenly, a light bulb goes off in your* head:

"They're *talking* about me!"

You are imagining persecution. Recognize this as coming from the Devil- a lying spirit bringing devilish enlightenment!

Then the Devil "enlightens" all the people in the room, telling each of them that the others are talking about them. Each one starts thinking: I'll bet so-and-so said such-and-such because *of* so-and-so; and I'll *bet* such-and-such happened. This is devilish wisdom, and it instantly produces strife and confusion.

Refuse to listen to this kind of enlightenment. If you do what Jesus said, you won't get a persecution complex. Take heed that the light which comes to you is not darkness.

Make a clear distinction between true persecution and a persecution complex. A persecution complex, or paranoia, comes from evil spirits lying to a person.

A word of knowledge does not bring strife. It only brings peace and the fruit of the Spirit. It straightens out situations. When God reveals something to you, He will show you how to deal with it.

Walk in the Light

If you know absolutely that persecution is there, then rejoice and leap for joy! Only the truth will deliver people from darkness. There could be darkness in people's lives that they don't even recognize as being darkness. When you are speaking the truth, walking in the light, the light will expose the darkness.

If everybody loves you and loves everything about your ministry, then you could be doing what the false prophets did: teaching things that tickled the people's ears - not telling them the truth! (2 Timothy 4:3-4.) In Luke 6:26 Jesus said, *"Woe unto you, when all men shall speak well of you! for so did their fathers to the false prophets. "*

You have to preach the truth! Not everyone will love you because not everyone wants to hear the truth. The truth sometimes hurts.

The next time someone acts as though he hates you, or doesn't invite you to his Bible study, or doesn't want to hear what you have to say, then rejoice! Be scriptural - that's what Jesus said to do.

The Devil can only know how you are coping with a situation by your reaction to it. You may be tempted to cry about persecution, but always remember: As long as the Devil can get you in a corner and keep you there, he has it made! You have to advance on him with what Jesus said about overcoming persecution. Do what Jesus said outwardly.

Rejoice and Leap For Joy!

Your husband or wife may be persecuting you. Your children may be calling you a religious fanatic. Your pastor may be persecuting you because you speak in tongues or because you believe in divine healing.

Instead of saying, "Oh, no! This is terrible!" you should say, "Glory to God! Hallelujah! I rejoice!" Then leap for joy as you praise God!

"Do you want to be scriptural? Do you want to release joy and overcome? Then start jumping! In leaping, you are actually acting in faith as if you were joyful. Once you start leaping in faith, joy will come!

Do you know what will happen? Something inside you will break loose! Joy will rise up in you, and the Devil will flee!

The next time persecution comes against you, remember what the Bible says. Jesus told us how to overcome persecution and paranoia: *Rejoice* and *leap* for joy!

You might not want to leap in front of your church congregation and it may not be wisdom to leap in front of your persecutors. Maybe you should just go into your bedroom, or private place, and jump before the Lord! But wherever you go, I believe with all my heart that we should be scriptural, don't you?

Jesus said to rejoice and be glad, so jump and leap for joy!

• • •

If you have been persecuted by relatives, friends, or enemies, pray this prayer with me:

Father, in Jesus' name, I thank You for the love of God that has been shed abroad in my heart by the Holy Ghost.

Because I'm born of love, I forgive those who have hurt me and bless those who have persecuted me. I will let no corrupt communication proceed out of my mouth concerning them, but I will only bless and do good to them.

Because I'm obedient to Your Word, I rejoice and leap for joy. I am filled with joy and exceedingly glad because You, O Lord, are restoring my relationships. Amen.

If you are being persecuted and harassed by evil spirits, then declare your freedom and direct it to the enemy!

In Jesus' name, Satan, I declare to you and your cohorts before God the Father, Jesus the Son, the Holy Spirit, and all the angels of God that I am delivered from the powers of darkness and translated into the Kingdom of the Lord and Savior Jesus Christ.

You have no right to harass me because I'm a child of the Living God. Therefore, this moment I bind you and put a stop to all your maneuvers and plans against my life. Go! Go! Go, in Jesus' name, and do not return!

I rejoice and leap for joy because I'm free. in Jesus' name!

Books by Annette Capps

Quantum Faith®
*Reverse The Curse in
Your Body and Emotions*
Removing Roadblocks to Health and Healing
Overcoming Persecution

Books Co-Authored by Annette Capps

Angels
God's Creative Power® *for Finances*
(Also available in Spanish)
God's Creative Power® *- Gift Edition*
(Also available in Spanish)

CD's by Annette Capps

How to Know God's Timing for Your Life
How to Harness the Power of Your Thoughts
The Parallel Plane of the Spirit World
The Mind-Body Connection
Tapping Your Hidden Resources
Quantum Faith®
Dreams and Visions
More About Angels
Healing
Realizing Your Dreams by Restoring Your Hope
Changing the Course of Your Life
How to Create Your Own Reality
How to Develop Spiritual Discernment

For a complete list of CDs, DVDs, and Books visit:
www.cuppsministries.com
or write, P.O. Box 10, Broken Arrow, Oklahoma 74013
Toll Free Order Line (24 hours) 1-877-396-9400

Reverse the Curse

In Your Body and Emotions

There are many wounded and broken-hearted people in the Body of Christ who are suffering in their mind and emotions. The battleground of Satan's attack has been in the mental arena. Yet there has not been any practical teaching that would guide people into mental and emotional wholeness.

This book will show you how to reverse the emotional curse and in so doing open the door for physical healing and miracles in believers' lives.

Doctors cannot reverse the curse of sickness. Only Jesus can reverse the curse and bring perfect healing and wholeness to an individual's life. Learn how to activate God's power in your body by speaking and acting your faith upon God's Word.

ISBN-13: 978-0-9618975-0-5

How does quantum physics relate to the Bible?
Can words move mountains?
How did Jesus supersede the laws of physics?

Quantum Faith

There are amazing similarities between the teachings of Jesus and the discoveries of the new physics, quantum theory. The concept of speaking to mountains and trees may not be religious metaphor, but laws of a new physics that have not been fully understood.

Jesus taught that our words are powerful enough to move physical matter. Quantum physics has discovered that subatomic particles respond to the observer.

In this book, you will discover that your words and your faith (beliefs) are unseen forces that affect everything in your world. You are the one giving substance to your world through words!

ISBN-13: 978-0-9618975-5-0